A Taste For Life

Dedicated
to those
whose soul stirs
with a reverence for life
ever balancing
the dream
and the reality

A Taste For Life

by
LAURIE HARPER

Sebastian Publishing Company
San Mateo, California

Published by Sebastian Publishing Company,
1327 Shoal Drive, San Mateo, California 94404.
Designed by Abigail Johnston.
Composition by HMS Typography, Inc.
Printed and bound by Delta Lithograph Company.

ISBN: 0-913347-00-0
Manufactured in the United States of America

Contents

POEM

There are no lies here.
Incapable of
removing soul from body
these are written
not for approval
but understanding.

Once thoughts
needing no shape
now words
requiring such form. . .
please read between
the lines.

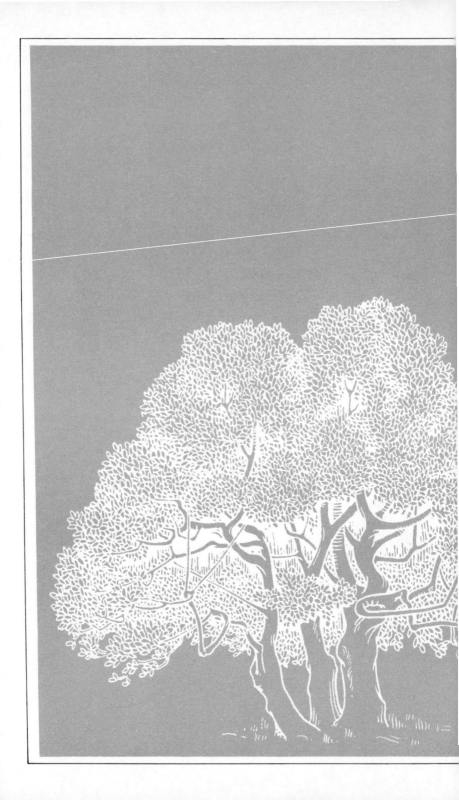

Friendships

With a knapsack of dreams
we venture out
of the snug surrounding
of family,
cautiously expanding
our radius of discovery.
The senses are alive
with anticipation,
our energy is unbounded.
We are too excited
to savor any moment,
until with great relief,
we find a friend.

FRIENDS

it's funny

i believe in you
more than you do,

and you believe in me
more than i do.

now we just need
to convince each other.

Our path is tremendously influenced and altered by the friendships we create or inherit. Friends share a common desire to heal and to be healed, through a mutual exchange of thought and emotion, through the joining of hands in a multitude of experiences. Utilizing empirical psychology, and balancing the demand for honesty with the need for approval, they test each other's ever changing attitudes and expressions while developing their life's course.

A trusted friend is like a fine priest, with vested authority to hear confessions of a most personal and intimate nature. The ability to hold these confessions sacred and private has bonded friendships or has crushed them. Like a priest, a friend is acting counsel amid struggles and decision making, often forgotten in the glory of success, but rarely omitted in the rationalization of failure. Nonetheless, a friend offers his own strength to draw on when we need to learn to laugh again, to dream a new dream, to re-establish direction and purpose. This dependency produces a depth and conscience that the friendship thrives on.

A true friend searches our eyes with a perception of the heart, and then cannot accept a lie. Our mirror, they become our enemy at times. Being a true friend is another version of being a parent. An agonizing responsibility with subtle rewards, it is a difficult and intentional thing to be a good friend. The rules and guidelines emerge as the friendship develops, through the thrill of understanding and agreement, as well as the painful disappointment of misunderstanding and discord. Over the weeks, months, and years that a friendship is born and grows, both people exchange parts of their soul, they help each other make crucial choices in their life, and they struggle together in the healing and inspiration of life.

Over time, we can get careless with it. We can get carried away with expectations among friends. We push the human limitations of each other in terms of patience, support, interest, and time. It can become history without ever saying goodbye. Some friendships are given away, we choose to let go. But longevity in a desired friendship needs the nourishment of new ideas, new problems and new experiences. A viable relationship does not survive on memories, on what was. There is high risk in being lazy with friendships. People change or move on too quickly for that. Each friend claims a particular place within us, and their absence will leave a noticeable cavity. The desire to remain an involved part of each other's life must be communicated, and the effort must be made. But the effort required is minimal compared to the rewards.

❦

DISCONNECTION

I know,

Sometimes in the very
moment of giving
something happens
and it doesn't come out
right.

It's okay, I'll survive
and besides,
you're the only one
who tried.

SEASONING

The creek is dried up
seemingly having misplaced
its content.
Backyard trees remain bare and cold
patiently allowing winter to prolong
their rebirth.

The illusion of early spring
is only the warm afternoon sun. . .
oh, that it were not.

So if I ask
if you, too, are a seasoning person
I do not refer to the
Spice of Life
but rather am merely hesitating
to admit
I have become as dry and cold
as this season around me.

PITY

You wear the same things
every day,
someone said
behind me.

We all wear the same things
every day,
I whispered
too late.

KINGS X

This hour,
there has been
declared silence.

Even you,
my trusted friend,
cannot help me.
I must pause
until the pieces do fit
and excitement reigns
anew.

Please just sit with me.

THE UNDESERVED

it just had to be
raining tonight.

the world sheds my tears
for those times
when caring is not enough,
when the tenderness of encouragement
falls prey to a game,
only to become twisted and ridiculed
in the ease of
disregard.

how i hate
to have a piece of my soul
taken and then thrown away.

i thought you were asking
because
you wanted to hear.

SURPRISE

How is it
that i know
you have not told me
the truth?
Because you gather others
around
when you need only speak
to me?

Does it bother you
so much
that i watch
your eyes and hands?

THE FOOL

Perhaps you have
misjudged me,
thinking me but an
emotional type.
But beyond the passion
lies a spirit of revenge
far stronger
than is wise.
Yet it being so,
do not think me
the fool
when on a distant path
my phrases ring in your ears
'til you cover them
in anger
yourself.

DREAMHOLD

Maybe
we should have let this
    crumble
when it cracked
the first time,
instead of plastering
a new hole all the time.

ONE & OTHER

So, my friend,
you shall stay
and settle here.
yes, it is fine,
of course very comfortable.
i've heard said
it is enough.

Yet never have they met
without parting
Enough & Not.
one knows not the other.

Whether
i wish you wanted more
or simply that i fear
becoming strangers
it doesn't really matter,
for you shall stay
and i shall continue searching.

❧
EROSION

i thought perhaps
time eroded
a cooled heart
as it does
the soil.

perhaps
there was a healing
power
in the
silence.

i did not mean
to hurt you
or
for you to die
before i could
confess.

TO THE KIND PHILOSOPHER

Whether it was your eyes
or your words
that gave me your meaning
i do not know.

But you are sincere
and i have heard you.

Your warmth was felt
through a winter jacket
when you hugged me farewell.

Thank you.

TIMBERLINE TIMES

Sometimes
one happens to find
a certain happiness
that is like a treehouse.
It isn't perfect,
sagging with aged wood or something
and you only love it slowly;
yet love it just the same.
There is a safety
in knowing it was built
intentionally.

It was very good
building this treehouse with you.
Some friendships
are hard to build.

HAVEN

When last bidding farewell
we knew
that inexplicable and necessary
changes
would occur
before we'd meet again.

Now it is
that, indeed, our appearances
have changed
with styles and haircut.
Yet the eyes remain,
only a bit
more so.

So we meet over and over,
recognizing each other
once again
and letting such moments
bridge time lost.

We have finally understood.

True friends enrich each other's lives
with a gift of themselves
that is separate
from any other form
of love.

The Search For Love

There is no greater dream
than the dream of love.
In that dream lies
all the love we can imagine.
It is pure and complete.
There is a fountain of happiness,
surrounded by an almost painful
tenderness and sensitivity.
It is so private and safe that it
cannot be touched
by the outside world.
It thrives on a bond
which is never broken.

CHESS

The king,
    a silent soul,
stands with his queen,
    of fine body,
while pawns
    of varying strength
make way for bishops,
    powerfully sly,
who dodge knights
    lying in wait
to stand enticingly close
    to opposing towers.

Surely this fortress
    guards me well.
such a marvelous way
    to await

Checkmate.

Our dream of love is born in secrecy, silently inspiring us to seek a life of our own. It is original, and it is designed to appeal to a very special person. We protect it, and it protects us. Seemingly simple in its demand, we are confident as we begin allowing others to enter our life, with all of its secrets.

We soon learn that the desire for love is universal. There is no one who does not seek to love and be loved. We all have a dream, no matter how deeply we may hide it. But the desire for love is not enough, it does not mean we are able to love, or that love exists. In love's many disguises we are easily fooled,

and our dream sorely tested. We begin to see
the many forms of love that are born of
impatience or deception.

Over and over again, we experience
variations of our dream of love and we are
forced to choose between accepting what we
have now, or going on in the belief that our
dream exists. Struggling to balance other
people's feelings with our own, we do not
want to destroy their dream, yet we must be
true to ourselves. There are no easy choices,
for it deals with the heart, so easily wounded
but so slow to heal.

Sharing someone else's life involves decisions
that call upon our entire being, not just our
dream of love. We assume partial
responsibility when we touch another's life in
the name of love. A common territory must
be established, and a common or
complimentary direction. The process of
joining two lives unravels our values, goals,
philosophies and convictions, entwined with
the dream of love. Sometimes lives do not
blend as naturally as conversation, and it is
only the promise that forces them to join. In
the effort to make it work, we can lose the
very love we sought to shelter.

It is a terrifying thing to make a mistake in love. We have a need to assume all guilt. But it is a tragedy to then create a means of living with that mistake. In fear we do this, believing it will save our integrity and reputation. We hope that by accepting full responsibility and sacrificing our own happiness our mistake will be absolved. We dare not consider any blame on the other person, at least, not until we have punished ourself enough to see that other side, until we feel our own wounds.

Love is a meaningful and worthy pursuit, though no life will remain unchanged in its path. Whether we find our dream of love, or whether we are searching for that dream, the effects of love touch both sides unavoidably. We are never the same person again, we are a better person. There is no script in love, and there is no timetable. But one thing is sure, the dream of love will only fade in the presence of a love that honors it. In the absence of that, it continues to challenge our choices.

INSTALLMENT LOAN

you shall know me
but only
a bit at a time
for you must repay
with interest
that which is borrowed.

and when all is over
we are forever
in one another's life.

i hope
to be of good credit.

MASTERPIECE THEATRE

One last curtain call.
This drama has served you well.
You have indeed articulated
that person you would have others know.
You have justified your self respect
in such a manner
that it cannot be denied.
The marvel of your accomplishments
and the strength of your victories
have been accounted for.

You may, of course,
proceed with my applause
though I will remember you sadly.
For I have never seen you at all
despite the evenings together,
and in this winter season
hearing descriptions of your warmth
will in no fashion
keep me from freezing inside.

VISITORS ONLY

How is your world looking now
that i have left you alone
with your treasures
and sorrows
which i could not be a part of
nor separated from

(never knowing when
 or which)?

Forgive me for failing such
a promising and well-planned time
together.
I just got tired of thinking about it
instead of thrilling in it.

I could have loved you
so very much

ECHO CHAMBER

Once surrendering
to desire the spoils
we are bound
in the tangle between
a bliss of belonging
and a struggle
to remain ourselves.

Once surrendering
to accept the easy,
the mirror holds no reflection,
only an echo.

WRIT OF ATTACHMENT

A bond is not formed
by the contract
as truth is not confirmed
with words. . .

Title, residence and phone #
have allowed us to become
too accustomed.

Please take the love
we originally knew
and return it to where
it will not be destroyed.
We no longer hold
what is asked in the above
name.

TRANSITION

We have had a thousand
conversations
since sitting down
yet not a word has been
spoken.
All your coffee is gone
and I did not see you drink
once.

What will you give
to get for yourself?
What will I give
to get for myself?
Love is not so unselfish.
Even with a compromise
it must still be
worth it.

OUR BOOK

How the aching inside tears at me.
To say goodbye is
to lay down an unfinished book.
I have not yet had time
to page slowly through,
absorbing it all.
I have only begun to learn of you,
to feel with you what you feel
and to love things for you.
I have never seen
your early morning face
to entangle in my image of you.
How does one end
an unfinished story. . .

THE FAREWELL UNSAID

i don't remember now
how you became
Everything.
it doesn't matter,
you were such a nice surprise.
that you left
i do not question.
but why did i not know
it was our last touch
this morning?

❦
YOU

hearing
this particular music
touches
those thoughts
i had so hoped could rest
while
i filled the empty space
with
whatever i could. . .

AFTERTHOUGHTS

If I ask
what it was that you wanted
from our love
it isn't to blame you.
It is one of the many questions
I must ask
while present becomes past
and I learn to see this
not as a mistake
but rather a step towards
understanding
what I can give
of myself.

SILENT SCULPTOR

why did i
so strongly sense
an outside carving
in this love
despite the tenderness
with which it was held. . .

perhaps time
had us out of balance
or even we, ourselves,
wishing us
earlier or later.

please
do not regret
though
the blade was sharper
and more swift
than intended.

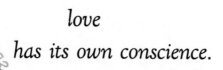

love
has its own conscience.

love
has its own justice.

Solitude

Solitude,
like darkness,
is a world of shadows.
As our eyes become accustomed,
the strangeness disappears,
and we fill the ringing silence
with our thoughts.

A.M. HOURS

I embrace the morning
because it is surely worthy
of my sleepy trust,
lingering to assure me
of its freshness.

I love the morning
because it knows
i have a chance,
not yet having done anything
i regret.

I cling to the morning
because it is frightening
letting go of
dreams.

Solitude has a place among our dreams.
A giver, not a taker, it is a salvation when
we begin to lose our perspective, when we feel
ourself becoming numb. Solitude rejuvenates
the senses that become faint and weary.

Sometimes solitude is unexpected and we
are overwhelmed with loneliness. One step at
a time, we gradually yield to the soothing
power of silence and become receptive to its
tranquility and harmony. Slowly, our
loneliness gives way to a relief, and a new
freedom is born.

Solitude is essential in the midst of
transition, with decisions made but results

not yet apparent. Committed to a change, we have forfeited our established security and there is a period of limbo between the old and the new. This is a time for reflection and dedication. We justify the present by examining our past, reliving all that has transpired to bring us to this point in our life. Alone, we are free to let our confusions escape, to let illusion and reality dance before us while we search within to confirm the choices we have made.

Solitude, intentional or not, is a necessary therapy along the path of discovery. It enables us to recognize a pattern and a continuity in our life, clearly defining our strengths and weaknesses, our values and sensitivities. We draw from it the reinforcement we need to make our decisions and to stand by them.

FREEDOM WINGS

Weather
is of such little
consequence to seagulls.

They kiss the wind
and scoff at rain,
while we dash indoors
to marvel at their beauty
and dream of flight
from behind a window pane. . .
safe, but oh so
restless.

Security
remains the obstacle
of all change.

GREENMONT ROAD

It is so strange
to lose my way
after knowing myself
so many years.
Right now
the drifting clouds,
speeding jets and road signs
make me homesick. . .
but for where
I do not know.

EARLY MORNING WEAKNESS

Lately
morning has been coming
before I am ready.
I sit up
to some music,
unable to think.
I cannot tell if my dreams
are real,
more real than my sleep.

Though I am no longer
afraid of myself,
this is a sign
that I am not yet
strong enough.

SUNSET MOURN

It's the kind of moment
one begs the day to stay
a while longer.

There is so much unfinished.

But the clouds are turning pink
as they slowly separate,
and the sun will soon
be turning out the light.

I cannot waste a single day.

WINTER TREASURE

Quietly closing the door
listening for the latch to catch,
the room welcomes me
inviting an evening of candlelit glow.

The world is locked out,
the curtains have been drawn
leaving only a still, shadowed profile
to reflect for outside lovers.

The warmth of this room
opens the soul to bare confusion
There will be no revealing
of thoughts that escape in whispers,
carelessly.

Nothing can be stolen
while much is given
in the silent echoes
of snowfall.

Solitude takes us
like a tarnished gem,
and polishes us until we shine
once again.

The Spirit of Life

The taste for life is an acquired taste.
A sampling of its quality
leaves us with a craving
for more,
and this is captured by
the spirit of life,
to become an inseparable
part of us.

ALMOST

There it was

A song on the radio
Holding a needlepoint near finish
With fresh, black coffee
At three o'clock rainy thursday.

A single, unrelated moment

So gentle in its presence
Nothing out of balance
Lingering in perfection
To be recognized.

It was nearly enough.

When the spirit of life moves within us, it is like the shadow of a cloud crossing over us. Its touch is distinct and its voice familiar. In a split second we experience a wave of both joy and longing, and we are overcome with the sensation. It has reached into a dream and awakened a thought, tantalizing and provoking us like a child who demands our attention.

There are times we must silence the spirit. When we are in the process of making a place for ourself in the social structure around us we must direct our attention to acquiring the knowledge and experience that will ensure us a comfortable existence. But the spirit does not die, it surfaces again and again throughout life, defying existence to be an end in itself. It protects the dreams we cannot forget, keeping them fresh in our mind. The spirit proposes to be guided by experience rather than stifled by it, and the spirit does not despair. We will always have another chance.

The spirit of life is a balance between ourselves and the world around us, between our dreams and reality. More than anything else, the spirit dictates a value to life, and seeks respect for this. As we struggle to understand ourselves and to believe in ourselves, we cannot afford to ignore the spirit. It is the one flame we do not want smothered, for the spirit leads us to treasures we would not find without it.

❧
APRIL

Spring has touched us
after a long winter's spell.
The windows are swung wide,
the sun sneaking into
every corner,
beef stew is simmering
and the fridge is finally defrosted.
Spring is always new.
The beaches are preying on me
while jets fill my head
with exotic daydreams.
I need everything,
I so want to experience it
always.

WOMB

My lovely earth

you have always known
how to wipe away my tears
with the warmth of your sunshine,
to tease me
with your fireworks of color,
and to soften me
with the poetry of flowers.

you know when
my glitter is fading
and you immerse me in your
change of season,
cleverly distracting me
with changes everywhere.

And so i return
in pain and in joy
to wrap myself around you
like a child in his mother's arms,
peaceful,
rocking gently in your winds
and surrounded
by your touch.

SUNDAY ALBUM

Helplessly treasuring those moments
when the sun catches
a reflection of the past,
i set aside my thoughts
and remember . . .

In every picture lies
a dream,
some long-buried
but a few still burning,
still waiting.

❧ FENCING

Indeed
the sword points at your neck
and our bodies stand
in defense
with forefoot placed
for attack.

Our hesitations are but
a preliminary to a stronger
thrust.

And so this life
exists
ready to retreat
but far more intent on
the advance.

We each have
our masks and armor.
It is a matter
of cause and skill.
There is to be a winner
though it cannot always be
he whose sword draws blood.

Life's most rewarding challenge
lies in defeating
the temptation to merely exist.

The Dream of Love

The dream of love
    survives the seasons,
expanding to unite all facets of life.
A captive of this dream,
we pursue it as a single course,
the strain of quality
    sought throughout.
Yet it is with incredible surprise
that one day,
we find that dream.

MIRACLES

I believe in miracles
because I believe in dreams.
I believe in dreams
because they free me.

I do this because I have to,
but you. . .
you were a miracle
I wasn't counting on.

Our dream of love is no more than all the love we hold inside ourself, the love we are capable of giving and the love we aspire to be worthy of. If we believe in that love as we believe in ourself, we accept the consequences of seeking nothing less.

Unlike love that is one-sided, or derived at by concession, this love is between two people who come together with a magic of miracles. With an honesty no less than we have to ourself, the backgrounds unfold to bring forth an uncanny likeness, despite the difference in lives. Like petting a strange animal, this love touches gently and carefully, made safe with the whisper of honor and respect. It explores the photo albums and boxes that lie in the attic, strengthening the love with trust and friendship. It encompasses the spirit of life and joins in the celebration of life. A unity forms without forethought, without struggle, as the dream of love is realized.

With a dynamic force of its own, this love does not stagnate. Like a newborn child, it is cared for, nurtured, and above all, cherished. A treasure for which we sacrifice, it is a love affair that cannot be threatened, cannot be violated. There was a price for this love, and it was paid in the absolute belief that our dream of love exists, as truly as the life we have come to value.

KNIGHTS

I wanted the Knight
to make noise with his armor,
his shield reflecting the daylight
while riding the strongest horse. . .

Alas,
this was for poetry.
He came to me gently,
and touched me deeply,
his life
reflecting the daylight
and the Knight.

SPELLBOUND

Please know why
I am here.
There will be no words
though the sound is sweet.

It has been a long journey.

As I hold you to my heart
whereby I look you in the eye,
I am yours.
Spells were never broken without words.
Let me be silent with you.

NOVEMBER TUESDAY

lie still
we are alone.
let me stroke your shoulders
and caress you.
let your eyes close to feel
the touch.
your needs
have been spoken
with no words
and myself i have seen
in your eyes.
there is no sacrifice needed
nor explanations.
let me be gentle.

i will not betray you.

❧
NEW

Nighttime
never used to be
my favorite time
until now,

when i've grown accustomed
to lying next to you
with my head on your chest
hearing your heartbeat
and our legs all tangled
to keep warm.

Nighttime
never used to be
my favorite time
until now,

when we whisper
so as not to wake
our unborn children.

REPEAT PERFORMANCE

No matter how strong we are
or how close we become
the question remains.
In silent, sleepless dawns
we wonder
what happened to old lovers.
A secret well kept,
not because of its importance
but because the answer
is so out of our context.
You needn't answer me
when I ask,
it is only that I don't want
to remind you of anyone
but Me.

SOMETIMES

it's not that
you did anything
to hurt me

it's that
i tried to wait so patiently
for you to finish what you were doing
so that
you could come to me peacefully
and i could make love to you.

but
you came to me too tired
and too distant
only saying goodnight.

i didn't even get the chance
to tell you how much
i love you.

AFTER MIDNIGHT

Lying next to me
you have not stirred
though I kiss your back,
though I hold you close.
Dreams have taken you
and they hold you
unaware
that I long
for your attention.
The confines of daily duties
have kept us busy
with no time
for the touch of love
we know so well.
It is not beyond us,
but being after midnight
and your sleep very deep,
you do not hear me whispering,

Come away with me.

CE QUI EST BEAU

Quand j'étais petite
j'ai pris des fleurs
doucement
pour les garder toujours. . .
elles sont mort quand-même.

Maintenant,
un peu plus grande,
je te prends
doucement,
pour te garder toujours. . .
Et même si tu ne meurs pas,
tu me montres
comme c'est difficile de toucher
sans blesser.

CRYSTAL

I don't think
we are as fragile
as we often feel.
Some crystal
has lasted a family's
lifetime.
Don't fear time.

FINALE

It is only now
that i can celebrate
all that has
preceded you,
for now it plays
together in a crescendo,
gloriously and triumphantly
delivering
the finale

i've heard inside me
all these years.

to find true love
we must follow
our dream

to keep that love
we must remember
the dream

and keep it alive.

STAINED GLASS MIRROR

Tonight, talking to myself,
I dust off impressions long left behind
to finally see a more permanent value
no longer distracted by reflections
of Now.

Indeed, moments cannot be discarded
having only served as reality.
Each is after a Before,
and before an After.
It is the magic of mirrors,
revealing not only who you are,
but who you are becoming.